ARIZONA
WAY OUT WEST & WACKY
THE PLAY

By Zachary Simpson

Based on the book
Arizona Way Out West and Wacky by
Conrad J. Storad and Linda Exley

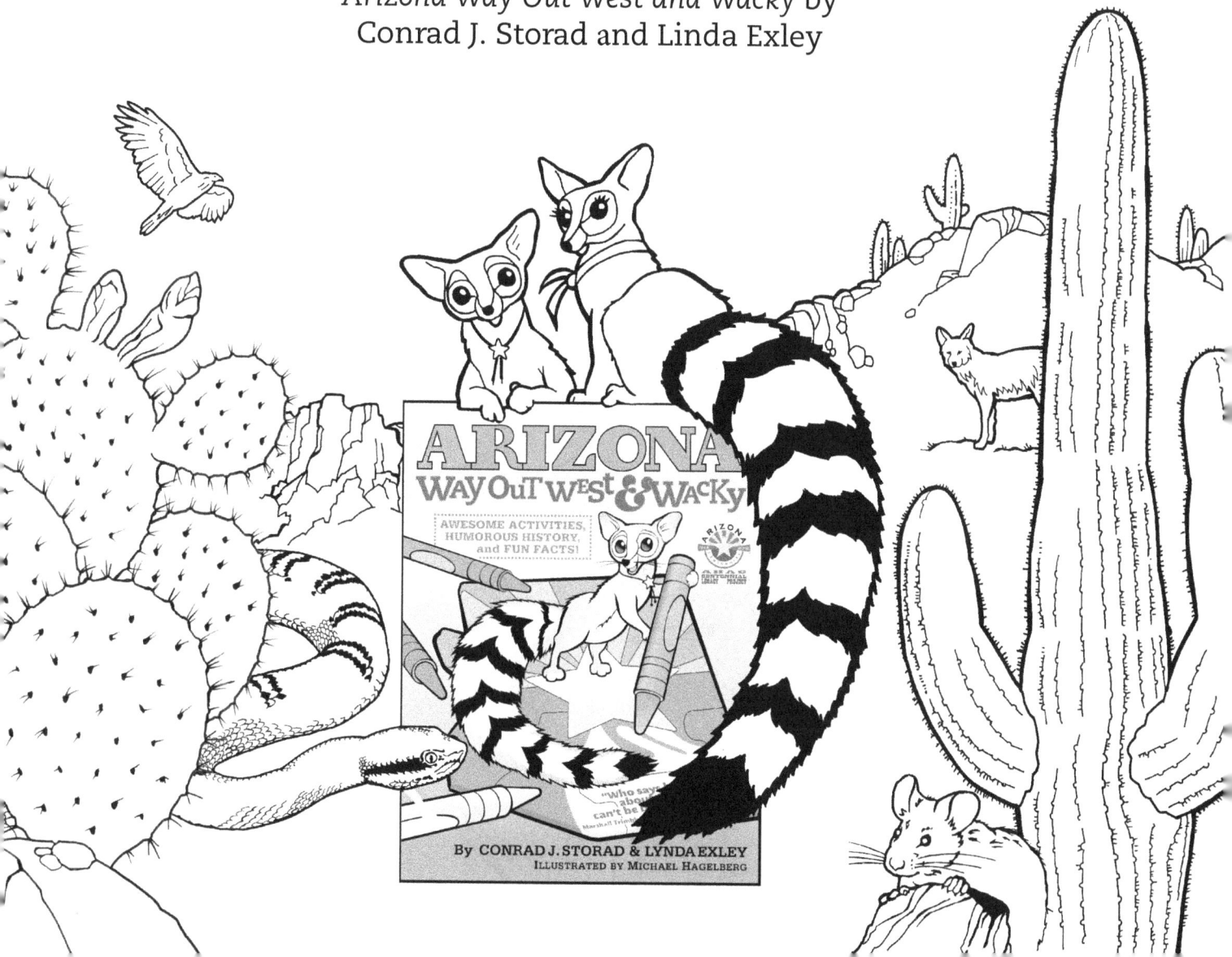

Linda F. Radke, Publisher
Story Monsters Press, an imprint of Story Monsters LLC
4696 W. Tyson Street, Chandler AZ 85226   480-940-8182

STORY MONSTERS®
PRESS   Publisher@storymonsters.com   www.StoryMonstersPress.com

Publisher's Cataloging-in-Publication *(Provided by Cassidy Cataloguing Services, Inc.).*

Names: Simpson, Zachary, 1991- author.

Title: Arizona way out west & wacky, the play / by Zachary Simpson.

Other titles: Arizona, way out west and wacky

Description: Abridged version best for grades 2 and 3. | Chandler, AZ : Story Monsters Press, [2024] | Series: way out west & wacky | "Based on the book Arizona Way Out West and Wacky by Linda Exley and Conrad J. Storad." | Interest grade level: 2 and up. | Summary: Join Ringtails named Johnny and Jayne Ringo on an educational and hilarious journey through the Wild West, from Arizona's earliest documented territorial days to its statehood in 1912. The play offers a perfect balance of learning and entertainment, with cleverly crafted dialogue, enthusiastic actors, and memorable characters. The play explores Arizona's past and present, sharing fascinating facts, amusing anecdotes, and touching moments.--Publisher.

Identifiers: ISBN: 978-1-58985-279-2 (paperback) | 978-1-58985-282-2 (hardcover) | 978-1-58985-284-6 (ebook)

Subjects: LCSH: Arizona—History—Juvenile drama. | West (U.S.)—History—Juvenile drama. | Cacomistle—Juvenile drama. | CYAC: Arizona—History—Drama. | West (U.S.)—History—Drama. | Ringtails—Drama. | LCGFT: Action and adventure plays. | Comedy plays.

Classification: LCC: PS3619.I56395 A75 2023 | DDC: [Fic]-dc23

Ebook: 1-58985-284-2(10) 978-1-58985-284-6 (13)
paperback: -1-58985-279-6(10) 978-1-58985-279-2 (13)
Printed in the United States of America

Author: Zachary Simpson
Book design and illustration: Michael Hagelberg

Hello Teacher, Director, Organizer, Parent,
or anyone looking to put on their own production
of *Arizona Way Out West and Wacky*!

We want to first thank you for performing this play. This play is intended to be as fun to produce as it was to write, while also giving your students/cast fun information about the state of Arizona. This foreward only aims to advise you on potential props, costumes, and the overall feel of the play.

However, the fun should really come in a collaborative effort with your cast to use your imagination when making the props and puttingtogether a wardrobe. The idea is not to have you spend a lot of money buying props or costume pieces but to have your cast bring the words on the page to life with their hard work. This should give them some proverbial "skin in the game" to also seek to put on the best production possible.

The options you read are just that: options. If you like them, please feel free to use them! And if you believe that you have a good idea instead, then go for it! These suggestions were compiled by me, the playwright. It's what I saw in my mind as I wrote the scenes and descriptions. I also don't claim to have a mind for practicality as it pertains to each production individually. So I aim to keep my ideas as cost-effective and fun as I can.

With that being said, I hope you and the cast enjoy yourselves!

THE PLAY (BEST FOR GRADES 2 AND 3)

This is a fun and simple production best suited for a younger cast. Hopefully, the comedy written in this play is more easily achieved by simply having the actors recite the lines. An adult saying these lines might be just silly, but a child saying them is what could be a fun delivery. The Ringtails can be directed on what to say by a parent or teacher assisting them along with each line.

Having the vignettes enter and exit while the Ringtails are talking is the best way to keep the play moving and avoid dead air. This will allow the production to stick to a short time frame and allow it to be added to another show.

PROPS

This is where the fun begins. The props for this play are intentionally simple and, in general, could also be pantomimed if resources are too slim. The fun in this is tasking the actors to come up with their prop. Show them what the actual object is and let them brainstorm on how to create that using arts and crafts. This can give them a sense of ownership over the production. Rather than being simply a character in the play they can stake their claim as the creator of the pickaxe or the clay bowl!

Here are a couple of tips for some of the props:
Ask the actors to collect toilet paper and paper towel cardboard centers that can be used for a multitude of structural objects.

Pickaxe Take one maybe two paper towel rolls cardboard center to create the wooden handle and then a third cardboard center to create the metal pick. This can be achieved by stapling the ends shut in a way to make it appear as the pick. Give the handle a brown paint job and the pick a gray one and you have yourself a pickaxe.

Phantom Mask Using a good stiff card stock of paper is all you need for your mask. The idea of the Phantom of the Opera's mask is that it covers half of their face and is stark white in color. That's all! So simply cut a round shape for the face, then cut it in half diagonally. Cut out an eye hole, and attach some elastic or string to each side of the mask to allow it to fasten to your actor's head.

WARDROBE

Most of your costume pieces can simply come from your actor's homes. Broadway-level costuming is NOT a necessity for this production. Using your best judgment and creativity will overall win the day.

Jeans Jeans will be perfect for several different characters allowing for a solid versatile costume piece. Miners, Frontiersman, or Politicians. All great uses of jeans.

Ringtails Jeans and a gray shirt are simple enough. Add a hat with some construction paper ears to give them the ringtail look. For the tail, you can aim to have a simple version. A grocery bag with crumpled paper in it painted black and white. A pool noodle cut in several different sizes with string poked through the end to then be tied around the actor's waist.

Miners & Frontiersmen Discolor an old loose white button-up shirt, or use a brown loose button-up. Find an old brown bucket hat or something similar. Add jeans.

Frontierswomen A simple dress will work just fine. Bonus points for a flower pattern.

Politician A black blazer, and glasses with a white button-up shirt and black slacks. Or jeans and a blue jacket with a white button-up and glasses. Bonus points for fake beards.

Family Casual clothing is fine!

Phantom Other than the mask, the Phantom will need a black cape, black slacks, and a white button-up shirt. That is all.

Cacti Green clothing is all you need. A green hoodie and green sweatpants are probably the surefire costumes for this role.

Cactus Wren The Cactus Wren has a combination of tan, white, black, and gray coloring. Where the belly is a tan that fades into white and a gray back and black dots throughout. Gray sweatpants and a white shirt can work for this character. Gluing or taping black construction dots around the outfit will give it the signature Cactus Wren look.

Tarantula The tarantula role will be one that will require a bit more setup, so this actor may not get the chance to portray many other vignette roles. Tan pants and a tan hoodie. You can create multiple areas with brown-painted pool noodles that are stapled or sewn into the hoodie. Add sticky googly eyes above the eyebrows and on the upper cheeks of the actor for the spider eyes.

In the end, all of these are simply suggestions. Improve on them, ignore them, use them. It's all an effort to make the production a fun and informative experience for you the director and the actors.

Make it your own and the fruit of your labor will come when you see the actors having fun with the material and your direction!

CAST OF CHARACTERS
(dramatis personae)

STAGE LEFT RINGTAILS

STAGE RIGHT RINGTAILS

PROSPECTOR

TAFT

MAN WITH FAKE EYE

COMPANION

KID 1

KID 2

PARENT 1

PARENT 2

PHANTOM

SAGUARO CACTUS

CACTUS WREN

TARANTULA

ARIZONA WAY OUT WEST AND WACKY—THE PLAY

THE RINGTAILS

THEME MUSIC PLAYS As the theme comes to an end, two groups of Ringtails enter the stage. They take their spots opposite each other on stage left and right.

S.L. RINGTAILS (STAGE LEFT RINGTAILS)

Good evening (Morning, day, afternoon, etc.)
We are the Ringtails, Arizona's Official State Mammal.

S.R. RINGTAILS (STAGE RIGHT RINGTAILS)

We are filled with knowledge and wacky facts about
the state that we call our home.

S.L. RINGTAILS

One fun fact is that we are sometimes called Ringtail cats,
but we are related more closely to a raccoon.

As this last line is being said a PROSPECTOR enters and goes to the center of the stage in between the groups of RINGTAILS. The PROSPECTOR carries with them a satchel or pack that they place on the ground.

PROSPECTOR

(To the Audience) I am a prospector mining for copper.
I bring my Levi's, pickaxe, and satchel holding my lunch
and coffee to the mines with me.

The prospector begins to pantomime using the pickaxe.

S.R. RINGTAILS

But the prospector's food keeps getting taken by rodents
in the mines.

A RAT tiptoes onto the stage and steals the satchel from behind the PROSPECTOR. The RAT begins to tiptoe off stage backward when one of the RINGTAILS from stage left or right walks over behind the right and scares them.

RINGTAIL

BOO!

The RAT jumps in fright and drops the satchel.
The RINGTAIL picks it up and returns it to the PROSPECTOR.
The PROSPECTOR turns and gives the RINGTAIL a massive hug.

PROSPECTOR

(With an arm around the RINGTAIL) **You will forever be known as my pet and I will call you my Ringtail Cat!**

ALL RINGTAILS

And that is where we got our nickname the Ringtail Cats

RINGTAIL

(With the PROSPECTOR'S arm around them)

But we are JUST Ringtails

The PROSPECTOR grabs their satchel bows and walks off stage.

S.L. RINGTAILS

With all of this knowledge, the only thing to do is to spread it far and wide.

S.R. RINGTAILS

So sit back, relax, and enjoy. . .

ALL RINGTAILS

Arizona Way Out West and Wacky!

Take a beat, and begin.

S.L. RINGTAILS

In 1850, Arizona became a territory of the Union,
but wouldn't become a state until 1912.

S.R. RINGTAILS

It was then we became a state on February 12th.
President Taft enters and goes to center stage.

TAFT

Wait, wait, wait! That is a national holiday.
It's Abraham Lincoln's birthday. It cannot be the 12th.

S.R. RINGTAILS

So we made it February 13th.

TAFT

Ohhh, wait, wait, wait. . . again. That won't work!
Thirteen is an unlucky number. It cannot be the 13th.

ALL RINGTAILS

So we decided to make it February 14th. The 48th state
of the United States of America.

TAFT

Oh, I love that day!

TAFT bows and exits the stage.

S.L. RINGTAILS

The question we now have is where the state capital will go.

S.R. RINGTAILS

First, it was in Prescott.

S.L. RINGTAILS

Then it was Tucson.

S.R. RINGTAILS

Then it was Prescott again.

S.L. RINGTAILS

But when Arizona became a state, there was a vote
to finally decide where the capital would go.

S.R. RINGTAILS

And it is a wacky story!

*Enter a MAN with a stool and a cup of water dressed in
turn-of-the-century clothing. He pantomimes taking out his eye
and placing it in the cup.*

S.L. RINGTAILS

The night before the vote, this man, with a fake eye, was getting
ready for bed.

MAN WITH FAKE EYE

Tomorrow I will cast my vote for Prescott to be the state capital
of Arizona, and that is that.

S.R. RINGTAILS

But the next morning his companion woke up thirsty.

*Enter a WOMAN dressed in turn-of-the-century clothing, who pantomimes
drinking the water. The MAN rushes in after her with one eye closed.*

MAN WITH FAKE EYE

Did you just drink my eye?

COMPANION

EYE *(Pointing at their eye)* did.

ALL RINGTAILS

Talk about hindsight.

MAN WITH FAKE EYE

(Overly dramatic) I cannot possibly let people see me this way.
I shan't be voting!

S.L. RINGTAILS

Prescott then lost by one vote and so. . .

ALL RINGTAILS

Phoenix became the state capital of Arizona!

The two bow and walk off stage.

S.R. RINGTAILS

From mesas to valleys and desert to forest.

S.L. RINGTAILS

Arizona's landscapes are all unique and beautiful.

S.R. RINGTAILS

But we aren't called the Grand Canyon State for nothing.
We have one of the Seven Wonders of the World,
and boy is it wonderful!

S.L. RINGTAILS

The Grand Canyon is over 200 miles long and 18 miles across
at its widest. If you wanted to drive from the North Rim
Visitor Center to the South Rim Visitor Center,
it would take about 4 hours!

*As the last line is being spoken, a FAMILY OF FOUR comes out to center
stage with two chairs. The "PARENTS" sit in the chairs next to each
other as the "KIDS" stand behind them making a makeshift car.
The KIDS are bored and disinterested and the parents are all smiles.
They all bounce to pantomime riding in the car.*

KID 1

Are we there yet?

KID 2

Yeah, I'm hungry.

PARENT 1

Oh, I'd say another two hours left so halfway there.

PARENT 2

It's a long drive but goodness is it pretty!

S.R. RINGTAILS

And that's if you drive! Fewer people have completed
a continuous lengthwise hike of the Grand Canyon than have
walked on the moon.

PARENT 1

(To the KIDS) At least you aren't walking this whole way.

KID 1

How much longer if we did?

PARENT 2

56 days, 21 hours, and 58 minutes.

KID 2

(After a beat) Take all the time you want.

The family bows and walks off stage.

S.L. RINGTAILS

And on that hike, if you chose to take it, you'd get the chance
to see all of the wonderful plant life.

S.R. RINGTAILS

Cacti are everywhere in Arizona. There is the Organ Pipes Cactus which can grow to be almost 20 feet tall and have 20 columns.

Enter a group of PEOPLE in green long sleeve shirts and pants followed by the PHANTOM OF THE OPERA in a half mask of white and a black cape. The green clothed group lies on their back and mimics an Organ Pipe Cactus, as the PHANTOM pretends to play the organ.

PHANTOM

(to the audience) Sing my angel of Musi—ouch!

The PHANTOM pricks their finger and runs off stage. The green clothed cacti stand up and all make different sizes of SAGUARO CACTI.

S.L. RINGTAILS

Standing up to 50 feet tall, with some over 200 years old, the Saguaro Cactus can be seen in the arid Sonoran Desert portion of Arizona.

S.R. RINGTAILS

Since they can store lots of water in their trunk, the Saguaro Cactus is used as a hotel for different types of animals and insects.

Entering the stage are a CACTUS WREN and a TARANTULA. They have luggage with them and stand in line before one of the SAGUARO CACTI. One of the CACTI breaks their pose to be a front desk worker at the very luxurious hotel known as Casa Saguaro.

SAGUARO CACTUS

Welcome to Casa Saguaro, your oasis in the desert. Checking in Mr. . . ?

CACTUS WREN

Wren. Cactus Wren.

SAGUARO CACTUS

Oh yes, my apologies Mr. Wren. We have the VIP room set aside
for THE Official State Bird.

S.R. RINGTAILS

Before we get ahead of ourselves, we should look at some
of the occupants of the Saguaro.

S.L. RINGTAILS

Yes, this is the Cactus Wren. It is known, not only, for being the
State Bird of Arizona, but for its very distinct and very loud call.

*The CACTUS WREN steps up and waves to the audience as though they
were a celebrity on a late-night talk show. Bowing and mouthing
"Thank You" in appreciation.*

CACTUS WREN

(To the audience) Oh stop, stop! No, you are awesome!
Yes, thank you, thank you.

ALL RINGTAILS

Do the call. Do the call. Do the call.

CACTUS WREN

Well. . . Alright!

*The CACTUS WREN calls as loud as it can while trying to mimic
the actual sound of a CACTUS WREN. Everyone onstage from the
SAGUARO CACTI to the RINGTAILS all cringe and cover their ears.*

CACTUS WREN

(After a beat) You are welcome.

The CACTUS WREN bows, retrieves their luggage, and exits the stage.

SAGUARO CACTUS

(To the TARANTULA) Next up. Welcome to Casa Saguaro,
your oasis in the desert. Checking in?

Timidly the TARANTULA slowly walks up to the front desk cactus.

TARANTULA

(Stuttering) Oh, um, hi. Room for Tarantula?

The rest of the posing SAGUAROS scream and run off stage.
The TARANTULA slumps over sad.

S.R. RINGTAILS

Though the Tarantula is scary to most people,
they actually have a timid personality and would prefer
to be in their hole in the ground.

S.L. RINGTAILS

They are friendly, but...

ALL RINGTAILS

Always use caution when around them.

The TARANTULA steps downstage to the audience.

TARANTULA

(To the audience) Sometimes I just get a little scared,
but I promise I'm not a bad guy!

The TARANTULA steps back to the Casa Saguaro front desk cactus.

SAGUARO CACTUS

(Giving the TARANTULA its room key) **Here you are,**
a nice cozy hole in the ground right outside.

The Tarantula lights up at the idea of a hole in the ground to sleep in.

TARANTULA

OH GOODY MY FAVORITE!

The TARANTULA grabs the key and its luggage and runs off stage.
The SAGUARO CACTUS follows.

S.L. RINGTAILS

There are so many more wacky facts about Arizona
that we didn't get to.

S.R. RINGTAILS

Maybe you can learn more at the next children's play you attend.
Until then, we hope you enjoyed our show. . .

ALL RINGTAILS

Arizona Way Out West and Wacky!

END OF PLAY

ARIZONA

Way Out West & Wacky

The Play

BEST FOR GRADES 4 AND UP

THE PLAY (BEST FOR GRADES 4 AND UP)

My idea behind several of the comedic moments can easily be summed up in one word: Pacing. How long is too long of a "beat" or for that matter, how short is too short? The answer also lies in a single word. Feel. When an actor takes a beat, depending on the context, you will FEEL when it isn't long or short enough. Experiment with this. Let the actor make that decision in rehearsal. Direct them to take a second before responding and to feel that space between when the previous line was spoken and when they are to say their line. As the director, you will know when it isn't right and you can go from there, but allow them the chance to explore this style of comedic acting. Some may surprise you and nail it! It will be a great learning experience either way!

Another aspect of pacing comes down to how quickly lines are spouted out. The beats, as mentioned before, are stated in the script. Most other lines should trot along with minimal pausing, or hesitation. These scenes should have a rhythm to them. For example: in the scene where Johnny and Jayne Ringo go back and forth labeling the different topography of Arizona, they do this with a rhythmic cadence. As if there is a drum set playing along with them. As the director though you should guide these young actors to a comfortable pacing, and don't get discouraged if they don't get it. Comedy is not easy. Create your scenes as best you can!

Johnny and Jayne Ringo are big roles with a lot of lines to memorize. It may be difficult to have young actors memorize all of this, so the idea of casting multiple Johnny and Jayne's to accommodate the heavy load is encouraged. Simply swap them out as often as you need. A good rule of thumb is to do so while the audience is distracted. For instance, when you have a group acting out the vignette. Unfortunately, as much as I would like to be there with you and help, I don't know your cast as well as you do. Some young actors have the skills to learn lots of lines. My trust is in you, the director, to make that decision when casting.

Speaking of vignettes, these were an easy ploy to comedically act out the information being spoken by the Ringos. Unless otherwise stated, these will take center stage when performed. There is no need to cast one person for each character. Someone playing an Indigenous person can also play a miner or frontier person. I had these vignettes entering and exiting opposite sides of the stage to allow time for the actors to change into the next character. Also if you do have a really large cast, you can have them be background actors to the vignettes.

One last thing about the vignettes. You never want "dead air," or silence, as the audience waits for the vignette to set up. Don't wait for Johnny and Jayne or Jo to finish speaking to send out the actors for the scene. Find a good spot WHILE Johnny, Jayne, and Jo are talking to quietly send out the actors to be in place and ready to go when the audience's attention shifts to them. Once the vignette says its last line, they can again quietly exit the stage. A lot of moving parts but it will create a solid production, I promise you!

THE CHARACTERS

Jo was named so to aid in casting. It is a neutral name that will allow you to cast whomever you want. The characters themselves are a way to progress the story. They aim to get the information they need for their report. Your typical kid.

Johnny is very excited about the history of Arizona. The schtick of the Ringos is probably his idea—through many attempts of trial and error—though it seems that he is still in the trial phase. He really just wants everyone to be as interested as he is. A desert cowboy of sorts.

Jayne is also very excited about the history of Arizona, however, she tends to approach it with maternal patience at times. She is the more level-headed of the two. A solid mix of debutante and cowgirl.

Vignette Characters Each character's identity is up to your interpretation. Some are more obvious than others, but if it's not explicitly stated, then feel free to do whatever you see fit as the director!

PROPS

This is where the fun begins. The props for this play are intentionally simple and, in general, could also be pantomimed if resources are too slim. The fun in this is tasking the actors to come up with their prop. Show them what the actual object is and let them brainstorm on how to create that using arts and crafts. This can give them a sense of ownership over the production. Rather than a character in the play, they can stake their claim as the creator of the pickaxe or the clay bowl!

Here are a couple of tips for some of the props.

We want this production to be as fun and low-stress as possible. Ask the actors to collect toilet paper and paper towel cardboard centers that can be used for a multitude of structural objects.

Cut Cords Simply take a chord from something, could be a power chord, or an extra HDMI chord. No need to actually cut it but the idea is that Johnny pulls it from his back pocket, looks at it, then throws it off stage. If it's an old chord that is broken or of no use, the effect of cutting it may add a little extra comedy to the bit.

Pickaxe Take one maybe two paper towel rolls cardboard center to create the wooden handle and then a third cardboard center to create the metal pick. This can be achieved by stapling the ends shut in a way to make it appear as the pick. Give the handle a brown paint job and the pick a gray one and you have yourself a pickaxe.

Dynamite Bundles Take 5–8 paper towel cardboard centers per bundle and cover each end with a scrap of paper. Bind it with glue or staples. Paint it all red. To add some authenticity, paint on a "TNT" in black on the side; freehand or stenciled.

Then glue 5-8 of your finished dynamite together then tie a string or twine around them, one on each side of the bundle.

Phantom Mask Using a good stiff card stock of paper is all you need for your mask. The idea of the Phantom of the Opera's mask is that it covers half of their face and is stark white in color. That's all! So simply cut a round shape for the face, then cut it in half diagonally. Cut out an eye hole, and attach some elastic or string to each side of the mask to allow it to fasten to your actor's head.

Tourist Binoculars Try NOT to use real binoculars. Use only cheap toy binoculars. Taking the possibility of broken expensive real binoculars off the table is always the correct choice. Aside from that, painting two toilet paper cardboard centers black and gluing them or stapling them together is all you will need. Add a black string or yarn to allow them to hang from your actor's neck.

Fake Snow Very simple. Cut up some paper into pieces. Easy peasy.

Famous Arizonans Simply print pictures of each person. Depending on the potential size of your audience, you may want to look into printing in a larger size than just a sheet of printer paper. Also, aim to find higher-resolution pictures online. This will result in more clear pictures that you print.

WARDROBE

Most of your costume pieces can simply come from your actor's homes. Broadway-level costuming is NOT a necessity for this production. Using your best judgment and creativity will overall win the day.

Jeans Jeans will be perfect for several different characters allowing for a solid versatile costume piece. Miners, Frontiersman, Jo, Politicians, or Rifleman. All great uses of jeans.

Miners & Frontiersmen Discolor an old loose white button-up shirt, or use a brown loose button-up. Find an old brown bucket hat or something similar. Add jeans.

Frontierswomen A simple dress will work just fine. Bonus points for a flower pattern.

Politician A black blazer, and glasses with a white button-up shirt with black slacks. Or jeans and a blue jacket with a white button-up and glasses. Bonus points for fake beards.

Jo Casual jeans and a T-shirt.

Rifleman Jeans and a blue jacket. Use heavy card stock to create military patches or ranking medals to distinguish the blue jacket from the politician.

The Ringos Gray sweatpants and sweatshirt. Possibly with a gray or black hat with some added construction paper ears. For the tail, let's get creative. Maybe: a black and white painted burlap sack with some pillows inside and a rope to tie around the actor's waste, or a long body pillow also painted black and white. The tail may require some creative construction, a great project for the actors to brainstorm on.

Indigenous People For this, we should aim to keep it simple. Tan or brown clothing of any sort. The actors for this vignette are only onstage for a short time so detail can be kept to a minimum.

Cacti Green clothing is all you need. A green hoodie and green sweatpants are probably the surefire costumes for this role.

Phantom Other than the mask, the Phantom will need a black cape, black slacks, and a white button-up shirt. That is all.

Trick-or-Treaters Let your actors wear whatever trick-or-treat costume they would like. Keep in mind, if they need to change for another vignette role, do not choose to make the costume too complicated..

Tarantula The tarantula role will be one that will require a bit more setup, so this actor may not get the chance to portray many other vignette roles. Tan pants and a tan hoodie. You can create multiple areas with brown-painted pool noodles that are stapled or sewn into the hoodie. Add sticky googly eyes above the eyebrows and on the upper cheeks of the actor for the spider eyes.

Cactus Wren The Cactus Wren has a combination of tan, white, black, and gray coloring. Where the belly is a tan that fades into white and a grey back and black dots throughout. Gray sweatpants and a white shirt can do a simple job. Gluing or taping black construction dots around the outfit will give it the signature Cactus Wren look.

Roadrunner The roadrunner can have a more caricature costume.
Running shorts, a tight grey athletic shirt, slimmer sunglasses, and a backward running hat are all you need.

Tortoise Similar to the Cacti. Green pants and a green hoodie. The big difference is to have a darker backpack on with a pillow stuffed inside to give it a full tortoise shell look.

In the end, all of these are simply suggestions. Improve on them, ignore them, use them.

It's all an effort to make the production a fun and informative experience for you, the director, and the actors. Make it your own and the fruit of your labor will come when you see the actors having fun with the material and your direction!

CAST OF CHARACTERS *(dramatis personae)*

JO	WOMAN
JAYNE	ROADRUNNER
JOHNNY	TORTOISE
MINER 1 & 2	PARENT (OFF STAGE)
COLONEL HARRIS	PARENT (CAR)
T–SHIRT AND SHORTS	PHANTOM
TOURIST 1 &2	SAGUARO CACTUS
TRICK–OR–TREATERS	CACTUS WREN
MAN WITH STOOL	TARANTULA

ACTS

1. THEME SONG OPENS
2. INDIGENOUS PEOPLE
3. ARIZONA FLAG, STATEHOOD, AND CAPITAL SEARCH
4. GEOGRAPHY
5. FLORA
6. FAUNA
7. FAMOUS ARIZONANS

1. THEME SONG OPENS

LIGHTS UP on JO. They are playing a video game on a TV. Completely consumed by it.

PARENT *(OFF STAGE)*

Jo, don't forget you have that report on Arizona tomorrow.
Time to call it quits on the Minecraft and finish your homework.

JO

Oh man, can't I just do it later?

PARENT *(OFF STAGE)*

No sweetheart. It's due tomorrow.

JO

Okayyyy.

JO turns off the television and heads over to their desk where a computer with some papers sit.

JO

(Speaking what they type) History of Arizona. Search.

(Beat) Whoa. There's a lot of stuff here. Hmm, Arizona Way Out West and Wacky? I'll click that. *(Reading the screen)* Did you know that the state mammal of Arizona is a Ringtail? What is that?

It's at that time the power goes out.

JO

Hey! NO! Come on! I'll never get my homework done now!

A tapping comes from JO'S window. They walk over to it and look through it.

JO

What in the world? Are those... Ringtail Cats?

JO opens the window and into their room come JOHNNY and JAYNE RINGO.

JAYNE

Well thank you kindly friend. I don't mind heights,
but JR has a little fear of 'em.

JOHNNY rushes in.

JOHNNY

(Brushing himself off) BLEH! I DO NOT LIKE IT
when we have to go to the second floor of a house.

JO stands there confused.

JO

Who are you? Why are you in my room? And HOW CAN YOU TALK???!!!

*JOHNNY and JAYNE hop closer to each other and stand straight
with prideful smiles.*

JOHNNY

Well, my name is Johnny Ringo, but you can call me JR for short.
And this is my kid sister Jayne with a Y!

JAYNE

Hello there!

JOHNNY

And you hit the nail right on the head. We are a couple of Ringtail Cats,
but most people call us Ringtails, from the great state of Arizona.

JO

So, you're cats? My mom is allergic to cats! You two HAVE to leave!

JAYNE

Now, now. Hold your horses.

JOHNNY

We aren't actually "cats." We are related closer to raccoons.

There is a beat as JO takes this information in.

JO

Then what's with the nickname?

JOHNNY

Well, a long time ago in an Arizona far, far away, prospectors would
keep us around in the mines to protect their dry food and coffee
from rodents. Heck, we became so friendly, they sometimes
considered us their pets. Calling us miner's cats, which then led
to the fun nickname of Ringtail Cats.

JO is still a little perplexed.

JAYNE

And we are here to help you learn about Arizona in an informational,
yet amusing setting!

*They do a small little hoedown and then strike a pose that signifies the end of their pitch
to JO. Then wait for their response.*

JO

(After a slight beat) So let me get this straight.
You two came to my house all the way in Nebraska to teach me
about Arizona for my report, which is due tomorrow?

JOHNNY and JAYNE smile hard and nod their heads.

JO *(CONTINUED)*

Am I dreaming?

JOHNNY and JAYNE exhaustively release from their pose.

JOHNNY

UGH! Jaynie, the presentation never works. People still
can't get past the whole *(Doing quote fingers)* "Talking Ringtails."

JAYNE

To Jo with more patience and ignoring JOHNNY

What my brother means to say is, no you aren't dreaming,
and yes, we are here to help you learn about our beautiful state.

JO eyes them both down. Thinking for a second.

JO

How did you know my power was out?

JOHNNY throws a cut cable off stage.

JOHNNY

A hunch.

JO shrugs all of this information off.

JO

Well if it can help me get my report done, then I'm all for it!

JOHNNY and JAYNE do a small celebratory scream to each other.

JAYNE

Great! Then to get started, all we need to do is go to the beginning.

JO

The beginning of the state? That must have been a long time ago.

JOHNNY

Oh yes, the statehood was quite a while ago,
but we will actually be starting at a time before that.

JAYNE

A time before the United States of America was even
a thought in someone's head.

2. INDIGENOUS PEOPLE

JOHNNY and JAYNE do a double clap and from the opposite side of the stage comes a small group of PEOPLE dressed in Indigenous garb. They are in a cave. Some are setting up a fire while another couple are etching petroglyphs and pantomiming teaching each other what they mean.

JO

Whoa, who are they?

JOHNNY

They are the Indigenous people of Arizona, long before your—
(Counts out 5 on his fingers) great-great-great-great-great grandparents were
even born.

JO

What are they doing?

JAYNE

Well, they are creating what are called petroglyphs. Archeologists
aren't exactly sure what all of them mean. They could be related to hunting or
religion, directions, or even star formations in the sky.

JOHNNY

What is even wilder, is that these petroglyphs are around
10,000 years old and have stood the test of time.

JO

Wow! So then Arizona became a state?

JAYNE

Not exactly. See, we will need to jump forward in time.
All the way to 1850.

3. ARIZONA FLAG AND STATEHOOD
AND CAPITAL SEARCH

JOHNNY and JAYNE do another double clap and the INDIGENOUS PEOPLE leave.
From the other side of the stage walks in two people dressed in 1800s POLITICIAN garb
and an old map of the United States up on a rolling wall. One politician pantomimes
pointing at the unlabeled area where Arizona would be to the other politician.

JOHNNY

In 1850, Arizona was admitted to the Union as part of
the New Mexico Territory. Then, 13 years later in 1863, it became known
as the Arizona Territory.

The two POLITICIANS shake hands and nod in agreement then walk off stage
with the map.

JO

Okay so now it's a state?

JAYNE

Not exactly. Arizona thought it would become a state 35 years later in 1898
by volunteering for the Spanish-American War. Pledging their loyalty to
the Union and proving they were serious about statehood.

JOHNNY

And after alllll of that, we finally became a state...

JOHNNY and JAYNE stand with pride and smiles

JOHNNY AND JAYNE

On February 12, 1912!!

JO

Oh, that's Abraham Lincoln's birthday!

JOHNNY and JAYNE slowly look at JO together in amazement for knowing Abraham
Lincoln's birthday.

JO *(CONTINUED)*

My state capital is named after him so I remembered that fact.

JAYNE

Yes well at the time, Honest Abe's birthday was a national holiday so they moved
it to...

JOHNNY and JAYNE again stand with an even bigger amount of pride and smiles.

JOHNNY AND JAYNE

February 13, 1912!

Then JOHNNY breaks the stance.

JOHNNY

But! According to President Taft, 13 was unlucky. So they changed it, yet again, to the now very official, will never be changed again...

JOHNNY and JAYNE stand in the same stance yet again, now with the most amount of pride and smiles.

JOHNNY AND JAYNE

FEBRUARY 14, 1912!!!

JO

Awww the Valentine's State.

JOHNNY and JAYNE break from their pose to continue.

JAYNE

People all over Arizona celebrated with fireworks, parades, and bell ringing! The celebrations were extravagant.

JOHNNY

(Chuckles) Yeah and in one place a little too extravagant.

JOHNNY and JAYNE double clap. PEOPLE in frontier and miner's garb enter from the same side as the Indigenous people did, carrying as many bundles of TNT as they can.

JOHNNY *(CONTINUED)*

In the town of Bisbee, folks were very excited to become a state.

JOHNNY, JAYNE, and JO all turn their attention to the group.

MINER 1

Uhhh, Jeb? Don't you think this is a bit much?

MINER 2 *(JEB)*

Nope. In fact, let's get a couple more bundles.
I want people to see the thing all the way in Flagstaff!

Back to JOHNNY, JAYNE, and JO

JAYNE

I don't know if they saw it all the way in Flagstaff, but the explosion was so large it almost blew off the top of a mountain. Now that's wacky!

The group of Frontiers PEOPLE and miners leave.

JOHNNY

Now what if I told you that the state capital was decided because of a glass eye?

JO

Something tells me that story is just wild enough to be true.

JOHNNY

Oh, and it is!

JOHNNY and JAYNE double clap and a MAN walks out on stage with a stool
and a cup from the same side as the two politicians.

JOHNNY

(As the man is walking out) See, in 1864 when Arizona was still a territory,
the capital was a town called Prescott.

JAYNE

Then, three years later, the title of state capital moved to Tucson.

JOHNNY

But then, in 1877, Prescott reclaimed the status of the state capital.

JO

But wait, isn't the capital of Arizona Phoenix?

JOHNNY

Yes, we're getting there.

MAN WITH STOOL

(Interrupting) Can you hurry please. I would like to go to bed.
I have a big legislative vote tomorrow to determine once and for all
where the capital will be.

JAYNE

You see Jo, this man intends to cast his vote tomorrow for Prescott
to remain the capital of Arizona. Before bed, he takes out his glass eye
and puts it into a cup of water, which is common among people
with glass eyes at the time.

The man fakes taking a glass eye out and puts it into a cup, and walks off stage.

JOHNNY

The next morning, his female companion awakes thirsty.

Enter a WOMAN yawning, she walks to the stool with the water.
She drinks the cup of water.

JOHNNY

(To the audience) Yep, you saw that right folks. She drank the man's glass eye.

The woman screams. The MAN comes in, still with only one eye.

MAN WITH STOOL

What? What is it?

WOMAN WITH MAN

I... Um... Accidentally drank your eye...

MAN WITH STOOL

Oh dear, I can't go out without my eye! It's my best feature!

The MAN and WOMAN walk out with the stool and cup.

JOHNNY

He never did cast his vote and because of that, Phoenix won the right
to be the state capital by one vote.

JO

That's crazy! And the state flag? I will definitely need that for the report!

JOHNNY and JAYNE smile, look at each other, and double clap.

*Enter from the opposite side of the stage a couple of people dressed in RIFLEMAN'S
coats. One holding a piece of fabric of some sort.*

JAYNE

In 1910, an Arizona National Guard rifle competition was being held in Ohio.
Colonel Charles Wilfred Harris, the captain of the team, saw that his squad was
the only unit without an emblem. So, he created a flag for the rifle team.

COLONEL HARRIS unveils the flag for his teammates.

COLONEL HARRIS

So I worked really hard on it but if you all don't like it, or whatever,
then we can, like, totally throw it away and never talk about it ever again...

JOHNNY

(Reassuring COLONEL HARRIS) Luckily, his teammates did like the flag,
and in 1917 it became the official state flag of Arizona.

COLONEL HARRIS

The design is simple, but I think it represents the great state of Arizona well.
The "Liberty Blue" at the bottom is the same as the national flag.
The rays of red and gold represent the sunshine that we constantly get year-
round. And the star in the middle is copper colored since we are
the largest copper producer in the United States.

His RIFLEMAN all applaud and they walk off stage.

4. GEOGRAPHY

JO

This is all fantastic for my report. I would love to have a section on the plants and animals from Arizona and maybe some geographic landmarks?

JAYNE & JOHNNY

That's easy!

JOHNNY and JAYNE double clap, and two TOURISTS from the opposite side of the stage walk out. They are dressed in visors, a backpack, shorts, and binoculars where they pantomime sightseeing and pointing to landmarks they see.

JAYNE

Arizona is a topographic treasure trove of mesas, valleys—

JO

(Interrupting JAYNE) Topographic? Sorry, I was asking about the geography of Arizona.

The TOURISTS stop what they are doing.

TOURIST 1

(To Jo) Geography is the study of all physical features on Earth.

TOURIST 2

While topography is what we call features on the surface of an area of land.

TOURIST 1

I think you'll want topography for your report.

JO

(Slightly embarrassed) Oh, um right. I knew that. Sorry about that, Jayne. Please continue.

The TOURISTS go back to sightseeing. JAYNE smiles, clears her throat, and begins again.

JAYNE

Arizona is a topographic treasure trove of mesas, valleys, and canyons. There is a lot of space for all of these features to lay claim as Arizona is the sixth largest state in the country.

JOHNNY

The state is divided into three main regions. Plateau, mountain, and desert. In the northeast, you have the Colorado Plateau, home to the Painted Desert, Black Mesa, and Monument Valley.

JAYNE

Close to that in the north are the San Fransisco Peaks, home to Humphrey's Peak. It towers over the city of Flagstaff at over 12,600 feet.

JOHNNY and JAYNE's exchange of topographical facts begins to pick up speed as they are going back and forth. The TOURISTS and JO look on in amazement.

JAYNE

To the east are the White Mountains.

JOHNNY

To the northwest are the Black Mountains.

JAYNE

In the center of the state, it flattens out near Phoenix.

JOHNNY

(Speeding up) Farther south and west is the Sonoran Desert, filled with shrubs, boulders, and cacti.

JAYNE

Oh my!

JOHNNY

(Speeding up) Head farther east toward Tucson and you'll find more mountain ranges.

JAYNE

Like the Rincon.

JOHNNY

Santa Rita.

JAYNE

Tucson.

JOHNNY

And the Santa Catalina.

JAYNE

(Speeding up) Chiricahua Mountains in the southeast.

JOHNNY

Sand dunes around Yuma to the southwest.

JAYNE & JOHNNY

Mountains, canyons, rivers, sand dunes, plateaus, forests, and desert. . .

JO

(Interrupting) Whoa, whoa, whoa. Okay, slow it down. I get it.
Arizona is a diverse and beautiful place.

JOHNNY and JAYNE are hunched over catching their breath. The tourists are silently applauding them before going back to sightseeing.

JO *(CONTINUED)*

You haven't yet mentioned the Grand Canyon.

JAYNE

Well yes, we obviously wanted to save that for last.

JOHNNY

Sometimes we get a little too excited about the topography of Arizona.

*There is a beat as JO stands waiting for them to start talking about
the Grand Canyon.*

JAYNE

Anyway. Some people call Arizona the Grand Canyon State
as it is located in the state's northwest corner.

JOHNNY

The Colorado River winds through the Grand Canyon. Over millions of years,
it etched the ground to create what we see today. It's 277 miles long and 18
miles at its widest point.

TOURIST 1

(To TOURIST 2) Hey did you know that the Grand Canyon is 6,000 feet deep?

TOURIST 2

(Amazed) No way!

TOURIST 1

The average teacher is 5 feet 4 inches tall.

The whole cast stops and looks at their TEACHER.

JAYNE

[Insert TEACHER'S name] How tall are you?

*There's a beat. The teacher doesn't have to answer.
The cast shrugs it off and continues.*

TOURIST 1

Anyway, with an average teacher's height, you could fit 1,125 teachers standing on each other's heads from the bottom to the top!

Tourist 1 is amazed with themself.

TOURIST 2

(Questioningly looking at TOURIST 1) Why would you use that metric as an analogy?

The TOURISTS exit bickering.

JOHNNY

And as diverse as the land is, the weather can be just as different around the state. Let's look at the temperature.

JOHNNY and JAYNE double clap and from the opposite side of the stage come two people dressed in a T-SHIRT and shorts, pantomiming the lovely weather of mid 60s.

JOHNNY

The state average is a nice, cool 60 degrees Fahrenheit.

TSHIRT AND SHORTS 1

(To their partner) Not too hot…not too cold. JUUUUUST right.

JOHNNY

Well remember now, that is the average.

The two people in the T-SHIRT and shorts immediately stop enjoying the weather and shoot JOHNNY a worried look.

JOHNNY *(CONTINUED)*

In June 1994, the temperature in Lake Havasu City soared to a nice and comfortable 128 degrees.

The T-SHIRT and shorts people pull out a squirt bottle and spray their face to emulate sweat and begin to fan themselves.

JAYNE

However, in 1971, Hawley Lake recorded the coldest temperature in Arizona's history at negative 40 degrees.

T-SHIRT and shorts people wipe the fake sweat off and get thrown large winter coats. They put them on and begin shivering while fake paper snow is thrown over them. After that, they exit.

JAYNE

But that is an exception. The sun really does love its time in Arizona. Though Florida is called the Sunshine State, our very own town of Yuma receives more sun than any other city in the country. A whopping 328 days of sunshine.

JOHNNY

And only a measly two and a half inches of rain each year.

JO

Yeah, Arizona seems pretty harsh. How does anything grow?

JAYNE & JOHNNY

We're glad you asked.

5. FLORA

JOHNNY and JAYNE double clap and a group of CACTI come on stage and pose as Saguaro cactus.

JAYNE

Arizona is home to a lot of trees, flowers, and shrubs that
you would find elsewhere in the country. However, cacti are found
in more abundance here than most anywhere.
These here are Saguaro Cactus and golly can they get big.

JOHNNY

And old!

JAYNE

Some can live to be almost 200 years old, grow to be up to 50 feet tall,
and weigh more than eight tons.

The TOURISTS from the Grand Canyon vignette come back out.

TOURIST 1

(To TOURIST 2) You know that would be eight giraffes.

TOURIST 2

Again. Why use that analogy?

They pantomime an argument as they walk off stage.

JAYNE

Anyway, they also have the ability to store a lot of water in their trunk
which is why they can thrive in the harsh environment of the desert.
Because of this, lots of birds, animals, insects, and reptiles use the Saguaro
as a hotel of sorts.

JOHNNY

Another cactus is known as the Organ Pipes of the Desert.

JOHNNY looks at the cactus actors.

JOHNNY

Ahem

CACTUS 1

(Hesitant) You didn't clap...

JOHNNY AND JAYNE

Oops!

JOHNNY and JAYNE double clap.

The CACTUS actors scramble to their backs with their arms and legs straight up to simulate the Organ Pipe Cactus. Enter the PHANTOM of the Opera. In a white mask that covers half of their face and a cape. He begins to pantomime playing the organ.

JOHNNY

Thank you! These cacti can grow around 20 columns
that are 12 to 20 feet tall.

PHANTOM

SING MY ANGEL OF MUSI—Ouch!

The PHANTOM touches one of the columns and pricks their finger.

JOHNNY

Yeah, be careful Mr. Phantom, sir.

PHANTOM and the CACTUS exit.

JO

Being able to survive in the desert seems almost impossible.
But humans and animals need food. How was Arizona even able
to become a place for people to live? Where is the food?

JOHNNY

Well, actually the Organ Pipe Cactus produces a fruit that is considered the best
tasting of all cactus fruits. The Pima, and Tohono O'odham people would travel
hundreds of miles to harvest them.

JAYNE

A lot of Native Americans from this region were able to find out what was safe
to eat as well as cultivate corn, beans, melons, chili peppers, and more!
The trouble was keeping food fresh in the harsh Arizona sun.

JOHNNY and JAYNE double clap. Enter a group of TRICK-OR-TREATERS.

TRICK-OR-TREATERS

Trick or treat!

JAYNE

A way for the Zuni people to prolong the freshness of their food
was to make a sort of wacky candy!

JOHNNY

They would pick the fruit off a yucca plant.

JAYNE

Boil it...

JOHNNY

Then peel it...

JAYNE

Pick the seeds out...

JAYNE & JOHNNY

Then have everyone in the tribe chew it up and spit it out into a bowl.

JO

What?!

JAYNE

The next day, the bowl of chewed fruit would then be boiled again.

JOHNNY

They didn't know this at the time, but that would clear the fruit
of any bacteria.

JAYNE

It would cool down. Then they would make small patties,
leaving them out in the sun to dry out!

JOHNNY

After they dried out, they would roll them up and the new dried fruit
would keep much longer than their fresh fruit beginnings.

TRICK-OR-TREATERS

YAY, FRUIT ROLL-UPS!!

*The TRICK-OR-TREATERS jump around with joy as JOHNNY puts some
fruit roll-ups in their bags.*

JOHNNY

You know, these trick-or-treaters make me think of Halloween
and spooky things.

TRICK-OR-TREATERS

We aren't scared of anything!

JAYNE

Goblins?

TRICK-OR-TREATERS

Nope!

JOHNNY

Ghouls?

TRICK-OR-TREATERS

Nope!

JAYNE & JOHNNY

Scorpions, spiders, and wasps?

The TRICK-OR-TREATERS all scream in horror and run off the stage.

6. FAUNA

JOHNNY and JAYNE have a little chuckle.

JOHNNY

Arizona is home to a bunch of wildlife including, well,
scorpions, spiders, and wasps.

JAYNE

Now, unfortunately, Hollywood horror films and Halloween decorations
have given the tarantulas a bad rap.

JO

I thought tarantulas are really dangerous.

JOHNNY

They are for sure and you should always be careful when
encountering a tarantula.

JAYNE

But, they actually have very shy personalities
and are very gentle creatures. Most of them would rather
hide in a hole dug into the desert soil.

An actor dressed as a TARANTULA solemnly walks on stage and hugs JO.

TARANTULA

Thank you for understanding me.

The TARANTULA begins to walk off stage and gives both JOHNNY and JAYNE high fives, This ends up sounding like the double clap.

Enter the CACTUS WREN, thinking the double high five was the double clap and thus their cue. They jump onstage and as loud and obnoxious as possible does a Cactus Wren call.

JOHNNY, JAYNE, and JO all flinch from the sound.

JOHNNY

Ah! Not yet Cactus Wren!

CACTUS WREN

Oh, I thought you double-clapped. That's my cue.

JAYNE

It is your cue, but no dear, that was just some appreciative high fives
from the Tarantula.

CACTUS WREN

Oh... My bad.

CACTUS WREN slowly walks off stage.

JAYNE

Well, the bit is a little spoiled now. But the Cactus Wren...

The CACTUS WREN again jumps out onstage and does another obnoxiously loud imitation of the Cactus Wren call.

JAYNE & JOHNNY

Not yet!

JOHNNY

We will call you when it is time.

The CACTUS WREN slumps defeated and exits the stage.

JAYNE

The... you-know-what is a common bird here in the Arizona desert
that has the loudest call known to Wrens.

JOHNNY

It is also the largest Wren species in the United States
which was criteria enough to make it the State Bird of Arizona!

JAYNE

Now JR, I think we might have hurt the Cactus Wren's feelings
by making them leave twice now.

JOHNNY

Yeah, I think all of us... *(To the Audience)* That means you too.
Should do the call to cheer them up!

JAYNE

On the count of three. One!

JOHNNY

Two.

JAYNE & JOHNNY

Three.

*The crowd and JOHNNY, JAYNE, and JO do the call and the CACTUS WREN comes out
with a large smile. Then does the call back to them. JOHNNY and JAYNE lead the
audience for applause for the CACTUS WREN. The CACTUS WREN does a bow and then
pridefully walks off stage.*

*Just then entering from one side of the stage and running as fast as they can to
the other is the ROADRUNNER. Running past JOHNNY JAYNE and JO, close enough
to spin JAYNE around.*

JOHNNY

Whoa, Jaynie are you okay?

JO

What was that?

JAYNE

Oh, nothing to worry about. It was only the roadrunner.

JOHNNY

(Not to anyone in particular, just out of frustration)
Is no one going to follow the double-clap protocol?

JAYNE

Well when you are as fast as the roadrunner, it's hard to wait for anything.

The ROADRUNNER again runs from one side of the stage to the other as fast as they can.

JAYNE

Roadrunners are Arizona's fastest birds but actually prefer to run
rather than fly as they can reach speeds up to 15 MPH.

The ROADRUNNER runs directly in front of the trio and stops.

JO

Aren't you going to say, "Meep, meep" or something?

ROADRUNNER

Legally? No.

The ROADRUNNER runs off stage. Passing the tortoise already "running" on stage in very slow motion. The TORTOISE is trying to be the roadrunner. But of course, It's a tortoise, so it remains in slow motion for the entire vignette.

JOHNNY

Oh, poor old man.

JO

Old man?

JOHNNY

That right there is the Old Man of the Desert. The tortoise.

JO

He's so slow.

JOHNNY

Yes, He is definitely not a speedster.

JO

How can he defend himself if he's that slow?

The TORTOISE is VERY slow. Not even halfway across the stage. But is acting like it is running very fast.

JOHNNY

Well, when in danger, the tortoise can hide in their hard shell,
staying away from predators that look to harm him.

JAYNE

He has a sharp and serrated jaw that allows him to shred tough grass
and other vegetation. That is where he gets some of his moisture.
Though he does take long drinks of water when he can find it and stores
it in a special sack inside his shell.

The TORTOISE is still not quite halfway across the stage.

JO

Wow. He really is very slow.

JOHNNY and JAYNE look at their nonexistent watches.

JOHNNY

Okay, Mr. Tortoise, that's all we have for you.

JAYNE

The show is only so long.

Undeterred, the TORTOISE commits to its slow speed.

JOHNNY

(to Jayne) We really need to continue.

JOHNNY JAYNE and JO continue on, ignoring the TORTOISE who is committed to the speed they are at and will get off stage eventually.

JAYNE

Right, okay so let's recap. We talked about the indigenous people.

JO

Yes, and the petroglyphs they made and how old they are.

JOHNNY

And we went over when Arizona became a state.

JO

February 12th ...

JOHNNY

(Correcting JO) 13th...

JAYNE

(Correcting JOHNNY) NO, 14TH.

JO

Oh yeah, the Valentine's State.

JAYNE

We went over the flag and how the state capital was chosen

JO

(Shaking off the grossness) BLEH! The glass eye.

JOHNNY

We went over the geography...

JO

(Correcting JOHNNY) Topography.

JOHNNY

Topography of Arizona…

JAYNE

And some of the plants, animals, and insects.

JO

Yep, that's about everything, right?

JAYNE

Not exactly. There are plenty of famous Arizonans that you might want
to mention in your report!

JO

Oh, awesome!

*By this time the TORTOISE is now about off-stage. JOHNNY, JAYNE, and JO all watch
the tortoise who right before exiting the stage stop and begin to turn around to make
another pass at the stage.*

JAYNE JOHNNY AND JO

GET OFF THE STAGE!

TORTOISE

Oh sorry.

He walks off the stage at a normal human pace.

7. FAMOUS ARIZONANS

*JOHNNY and JAYNE double clap and a line of ACTORS holding something behind their back
make their way onstage. They stand in a row.*

*JOHNNY, JAYNE, and JO go to the leftmost actor in the line. And begin to announce each
person like a game show host.*

JAYNE

There are MANY famous people from Arizona, so we will be going through
a couple of them. First up, we have Emma Stone!

The first person in line reveals a picture of Emma Stone from behind their back.

JO

Oh I loved her in *The Amazing Spiderman.*

JAYNE

Yes! Born in Scottsdale, she has been in numerous films and even won
an Oscar for her role in *La La Land*!

JOHNNY JAYNE and JO move to the next person in the line.

JOHNNY

Another famous Arizonan, born in Casa Grande, Joe Jonas
of the Jonas Brothers!

The actor reveals a picture of Joe Jonas.

JO

Oh yes, my older sister liked the Jonas Brothers when I was younger.

JOHNNY JAYNE and JO move to the next actor.

JAYNE

Next up, from Phoenix, we have Stevie Nicks!

The actor reveals a picture of Stevie Nicks.

JO

Ohhhh. Who?

JAYNE

Stevie Nicks. From Fleetwood Mac?

JO

What?

JAYNE

That might be more for your parents. Next up!

JOHNNY and JAYNE move JO to the next actor.

JOHNNY

Wonder Woman herself, also from Phoenix, Lynda Carter!

The actor reveals a picture of Lynda Carter.

JO

Don't you mean Gal Gadot?

JOHNNY

No no, the original Wonder Woman.

JO

Oh, sorry I think I am a little young to know her.

JOHNNY

Oh right.. Umm

JOHNNY and JAYNE move JO to the next actor.

JAYNE

Marty Robbins?

The actor reveals a picture of Marty Robbins. JO simply shakes their head. JOHNNY motions to JAYNE to keep JO moving.

JOHNNY

Famous Jazz Cat Charles Mingus?

The actor reveals a picture of Charles Mingus. JO shakes their head again. JOHNNY waves JAYNE on again. They all move to the next actor.

JAYNE

Michelle Branch?

The actor reveals a picture of Michelle Branch, JO shakes their head again.

JOHNNY and JAYNE move to the last actor.

JOHNNY

Okay, finally Cesar Estrada Chavez?

Actor reveals a picture of Cesar Chavez.

JO

Oh, actually I have heard that name!

JOHNNY

Really?

JO

No.

JOHNNY facepalms.

JAYNE

(Again more patient than JOHNNY) Well, Cesar is someone
you should know. Born near Yuma in 1927. Cesars family owned a farm until
the Great Depression which resulted in them losing the farm. He and his family
continued to work on farms following the seasons across the southwest
picking a number of different fruits and vegetables.

JOHNNY

He learned the hardships that came with farm workers
and in 1962 helped found the National Farm Workers Association,
which became the United Farm Workers.

JO

Oh wow. What is that?

JAYNE

It's a workers union that would help to protect the rights
of migrant farm workers everywhere!

JAYNE & JOHNNY

(in their best game show announcer voices)
And that is Who's Famous From Arizona!

The line of actors all bow and walk off stage.

JO

Well, that is more than enough information to get an Easy A on my report!

JAYNE

And honestly, there is still so much more to find out!

JOHNNY walks over to JO.

JOHNNY

(Hands Jo AZWOWW) Here. If you ever want more information read this.

JO shows the book to the audience.

JO

Thanks JR. And thank you, Jayne.

JAYNE

You betcha! I think it is time for us to go. If you ever want to chat
about Arizona again, all you have to do is get assigned a school report
about Arizona and have your power go out suddenly,
and have no way of learning about the state otherwise.

JOHNNY

If it happens again. We will be there.

JO

Yeah. Strange how it all worked out.

JAYNE & JOHNNY

(To each other) Right. Strange.

PARENT *(OFF STAGE)*

Jo, it looks like the power line was cut somehow.
We are going to stay at a hotel.

*The PARENT says this off stage right. JO looks to stage right to listen to their parent.
JOHNNY and JAYNE sneak off stage left while this happens.*

JO looks back at JOHNNY and JAYNE and realizes they have gone.

JO

(To their PARENT) Okay!

Thinking to themself, JO chuckles.

JO *(CONTINUED)*

Those Ringtail Ringos.

He smiles and exits the stage.

END OF PLAY

www.ingramcontent.com/pod-product-compliance
Lightning Source LLC
Chambersburg PA
CBHW081251040426
42452CB00015B/2788